HOME LIGHTING IDEAS

BEDROOMS AND BATHS

First published in the United States of America by:
Rockport Publishers, Inc.
146 Granite Street
Rockport, Massachusetts 01966-1299
Telephone: (508) 546-9590
Fax: (508) 546-7141

Distributed to the book trade and art trade
in the United States by:
Rockport Publishers
Rockport, Massachusetts 01966-1299

ISBN 1-56496-286-5

10 9 8 7 6 5 4 3 2 1

ART DIRECTOR
Lynne Havighurst
DESIGNER
Sara Day Graphic Design
FRONT COVER CREDIT
Appears on page 23
BACK COVER CREDITS
Appear on pages 10, 12 and 32

Photo on page 1 also appears on page 16. Photo on page 5 also appears on page 17. Photo on page 18 also appears on page 28. Photo on page 19 also appears on page 25. Photo on page 34—Lighting Designer: Claudia Librett, Interior Designer: Claudia Librett, Photographer: Durston Saylor. Photo on page 35—Lighting Designer: Linda Ferry, Interior Designers: Tony Carrasco and Greg Warner, Photographer: Russell Abraham. Photo on page 36—Lighting Designers: Charles H. Grebmeier and Gunnar Burklund, Interior Designers: Charles H. Grebmeier and Gunnar Burkland, Photographer: Eric Zepeda. Photo on page 37—Lighting Designer: Ruth Soforenko, Interior Designer: Ruth Soforenko, Photographer: Ron Starr.

Printed by Welpac, Singapore.

►HOME **LIGHTING** IDEAS◄

BEDROOMS AND BATHS

Randall Whitehead

ROCKPORT
PUBLISHERS

Rockport Publishers
Rockport, Massachusetts

Bedrooms:
Private Sanctuaries

A bedroom is the one space in the house that can be closed off from the rest of the world. This is the place where parents can get a break from the kids, and children can be alone with friends. The bedroom is the location where every day begins and ends.

The Way It Was

With a little ingenuity, the typical bedroom lighting scheme—a pair of reading lamps on either side of the bed and a light fixture centered in the middle of the ceiling—can be greatly improved upon. Begin with the ceiling: the popular white, glass pil-low-style light fixtures commonly used for lighting bedrooms have a glare factor that overpowers everything else in the space. Hanging, opaque luminaires, positioned a short distance from the ceiling, are a much better option; they use the fixture as a reflector that directs light onto the ceiling, thus spreading soft, glare-free illumination into the room.

Ambient Lighting

In bedroom design, ambient light should take priority. Ambient light is most flattering to people: it eliminates harsh shadows and helps erase dark circles and soften age lines. Try the hanging luminaire solution, or, if the space has a sloped ceiling, mount two or three wall sconces above the door. Using the "dead" space above the door has two advantages: sconces create great fill light from that position, and they do not interfere with wall space for artwork.

Tray or coffered ceiling designs lend themselves well to a perimeter cove lighting detail. The cove light helps emphasize the architecture, and fills the bedroom with ambient light. If you are reluctant to commit to an architecturally integrated lighting design, a pair of torchieres is a good option.

Another effective lighting technique for bedrooms is to place a halogen indirect light source on top of a tall piece of furniture, such as an armoire or a canopy bed with a solid top. On the tops of such furniture pieces there is often a recess, which makes a great hiding spot for an indirect source of light.

Task Lighting

In addition to ambient light, reading illumination should be included in any bedroom lighting design plan. If you choose the traditional approach of a pair of bedside table lamps, consider the following to get best results:

Select reading lights that have opaque liners in the shades. This will help direct the light down and across the work surface. Additionally, the opaque shade helps shield the light from one's bed mate.

Wall-mounted, swing-arm lamps are a flexible source of illumination that won't take up space on a night table. Height is critical to the success of these lamps: too high, and they create glare; too low, and the light falls in a poor spot for reading. Mount them just above the height of your shoulders when you are sitting in bed, and position the lamps so that light falls between the "work surface" (your lap) and your head. People sharing a bed may have different ideal lamp heights—make some compromise on either side to keep the lights even.

Another reading light option is to install a pair of recessed, adjustable, low-voltage luminaires in the ceiling above the bed. This is the airline approach to providing light for reading. You may have noticed that the reading lights in a plane are not directly over your seat, but actually over the seat of the person sitting next to you. That is because the airline designers knew that your head makes a better door than a window when it comes to light transmission.

Should Highlighting Play a Role?

Accent lighting is not as important in bedrooms as it is in other areas of the house. Still, there may be a special painting that you would like to enjoy in your private space. Using recessed, adjustable fixtures will keep the source of illumination hidden and let the art piece be the focus.

Special Effects

Some designers like to place underlighting along the edge of a bed. This modern effect makes the bed appear to levitate, and can also serve as a night light. Don't use undimmed cool-colored fluorescent lamps as a source of underlighting—they tend to make furnishings look like today's "blue-light special." A

dimmable fluorescent lamp in a warm color is a better choice. Low-voltage tube lighting (using half-watt lamps on 3-inch centers) is another good option: The tubing is flexible and bends around corners easily. The final effect should be a gentle glow of light.

No matter which lighting option you choose, the ultimate goal of bedroom lighting design is to create a warm atmosphere of sanctuary.

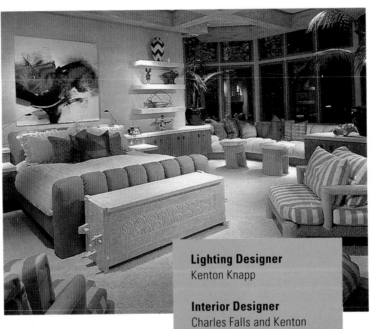

Lighting Designer
Kenton Knapp

Interior Designer
Charles Falls and Kenton Knapp

Photographer
Patrick Barta

Concealed lighting brightens this appealing bedroom.

Lighting Designer
Susan Huey

Interior Designer
Laura Seccombe

Photographer
Douglas Salin

This cobalt-blue light creates an incredible dream-like atmosphere for this frenetic sculpture. A remote transformer track system does the accent work while a torchiere provides the necessary fill light.

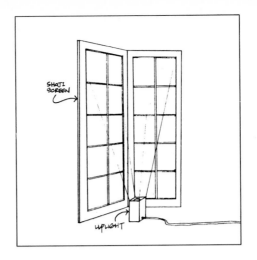

Lighting Designer
Marcia Cox

Interior Designer
Marcia Cox

Photographer
Russell Abraham

**This back-lighted screen
creates a warm corner for
the bedroom.**

Lighting Designer
Patricia Borba McDonald and
Marcia Moore

Interior Designer
Patricia Borba McDonald and
Marcia Moore

Photographer
Russell Abraham

**A neon squiggle adds punch
to this colorful kid's room.**

Lighting Designer
Linda Ferry

Interior Designer
Carolyn Hardy

Photographer
Douglas Salin

The sumptuous bedroom benefits from the illuminated trees beyond the window. The bay window almost becomes a living screen and complements the one behind the bed.

Lighting Designer
Kenton Knapp and
Robert Truax

Interior Designer
Charles Falls

Photographer
Mary Nichols

A huge mineral stone appears to be glowing on the foreground coffee table.

Lighting Designer
Don Maxcy

Interior Designer
Don Maxcy

Photographer
Russell Abraham

A rounded cove detail provides a pleasing indirect light. Wall-mounted reading lights provide excellent illumination without glare.

Lighting Designer
Randall Whitehead and
Catherine Ng

Interior Designer
Christian Wright and
Gerald Simpkins

Photographer
Ben Janken

**Glass block walls allow
light to travel from room to
room and help to get natural
ambient light into interior
rooms. Cantilevered wall
sconces throw light up and
out into the bedroom.**

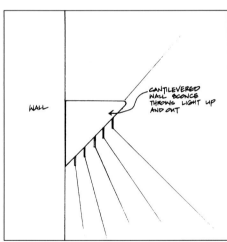

Lighting Designer
Robert Truax and Kenton Knapp

Interior Designer
Charles Falls

Photographer
Eric Zepeda

**Recessed adjustable
fixtures help create the
drama for this spectacular
penthouse bedroom.**

Lighting Designer
Pam Pennington

Interior Designer
Pam Pennington

Photographer
Russell Abraham

**For a high-tech look on a
low budget, the existing**
**fixture in the center of the
room was replaced with
two suspended bars onto
which the designer
clamped low-voltage
fixtures fitted with curly cable.
A red filter projects
a fanciful spot of color on
the comforter.**

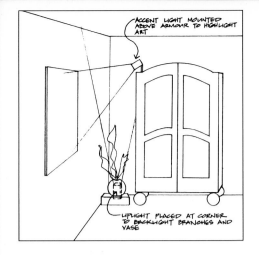

ACCENT LIGHT MOUNTED
ABOVE ARMOUR TO HIGHLIGHT
ART

UPLIGHT PLACED AT CORNER
TO BACKLIGHT BRANCHES AND
VASE

Lighting Designer
Randall Whitehead

Interior Designer
Lilley Yee

Photographer
Russell Abraham

Grace and style are enhanced in this view which looks out from the canopy bed. The soft effect is achieved by the artful placement of an uplight in the far corner which provides backlighting for the branches and vase. Careful highlighting of the specific details renders order to this elegant space.

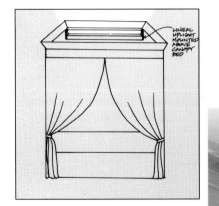

LINEAL
UPLIGHT
MOUNTED
ABOVE
CANOPY
BED

Lighting Designer
Randall Whitehead

Interior Designer
Lilley Yee

Photographer
Russell Abraham

This elegant canopy bed contains a surprise, concealing a subtle up light that sends a soft wash into the ceiling. A suit of armour is both backlit and side lit to reveal its form as a protective presence balancing out another character in this room, an accented statue of Cupid.

14

Lighting Designer
Michael Souter

Interior Designer
Barbara Jacobs

Photographer
Russell Abraham

A central fixture was replaced with a specially-designed box housing eight recessed downlights. They provide all the accent lighting the room needs.

Lighting Designer
Cynthia Bolton Karasik
and James Benya

Interior Designer
Colleen Roger and Don Simons

Photographer
James Benya

**Backlighted and forelighted
shoji screens add textural
interest to this bedroom.**

Lighting Designer
James Benya

Interior Designer
Sharon Marston

Photographer
James Benya

**Bedside table lamps
provide both task and
gentle fill light for this
luxurious master bedroom.**

Lighting Designer
James Benya

Interior Designer
Sharon Marston

Photographer
James Benya

A shell-shaped rice paper fixture adds visual interest to this reading corner.

Lighting Designer
Cynthia Bolton Karasik
and James Benya

Interior Designer
Gary Hutton

Photographer
James Benya

Wall washers at an acute angle show off the texture of the stone wall.

Baths:
Functional Luxury

Well-designed lighting is of the utmost importance in the bathroom. Yet, more often than not, people use inadequate lighting techniques for much-needed task illumination. How many times have we seen dramatic photographs of a vanity mirror with the recessed downlight positioned directly over the sink? It works for the photographs, but not for people. Standing at the mirror with harsh light shining down on your head creates the same kind of "horror movie" shadows that holding a flashlight under your chin does. This is extremely bad lighting for shaving or applying makeup.

Surface-mounted luminaires are only slightly better than the recessed models. At best, they illuminate the top half of your face, and leave the bottom half in shadow. This is an especially bad light for shaving, since there are only so many ways to tilt your head to catch the light.

Task Lighting

For the best task lighting, install two luminaires, flanking the mirror area above the sink, to provide the necessary cross-illumination. The principle of cross-illumination on the vertical axis originated in the theater, where actors and actresses applied make-up in front of mirrors surrounded by bare lamps in porcelain sockets. About 25 years ago, luminaire manufacturers began to put vanity light bars on the market in imitation of this technique. Soon, homes everywhere were sporting the now ubiquitous three-lamp brass or chrome bar above the mirror.

Remember, these bars work well only when they are mounted on each side of the mirror. A third luminaire could be mounted above the mirror, but it is not necessary for good task lighting. A luminaire mounted by itself, above the mirror, is not an adequate source of work light.

A more recent cross-illumination trend is to wall-mount translucent luminaires at eye-level on either side of the sink. These can flank a hanging mirror or mount directly on a wall-to-wall mirror. To reduce the risk of electric shock, any lighting located close to water should be installed with an instantaneous circuit shutoff, called a "ground fault interrupter" (GFI).

Many builders and architects have a propensity for installing fluorescent or incandescent light in soffits, fitted with either acrylic diffusers or egg-crate louvers, over vanity areas. These also tend to illuminate only the top half of the user's face. A white or glossy counter can help reflect some light from below, by reflecting illumination up onto the lower part of the face. This is a passable substitute if vertical cross-illumination is impossible to install. Remember, the more items that collect on the counter, the less reflective surface there will be.

While the task area at the vanity is the most critical, other areas of the bath also require proper lighting. Tubs and showers both need good general light. For this purpose, recessed luminaires with white opal diffusers are commonly used. A drawback, however, is that many of these units project several inches below the ceiling line and may shine in the user's eyes. A luminaire with a lens that is flush with or recessed into the ceiling is preferable for those who are sensitive to bright light. However, with such a fully recessed unit, the upper third of the shower or tub area will be slightly dimmer.

Fluorescent Fears

The fluorescent option is important today, because fluorescent lighting is at least three times more energy efficient than incandescent lighting. Several states permit only fluorescent light as the general light source in the design, construction, or remodeling of residential bathrooms. Fortunately, many of today's fluorescent lamps are very flattering to skin tones. In response to color rendition criticisms, most manufacturers have introduced recessed and surface-mounted fixtures that use color-corrected bulbs, including the newer compact fluorescents (CFL). The 13-watt version can provide excellent color rendering, and produces an amount of illumination equal to a 60-watt incandescent bulb. Many of today's fixtures even use a 26-watt lamp that provides as much light as a 120-watt incandescent source. And, since CFL's are available in a color temperatures close to that of incandescent lamp bulbs, both can be used in one room without creating odd color variations.

Lighting for Extra Elegance

Indirect lighting adds a soft warm glow to the bath. Wall sconces or cove lighting can provide ambient light reflected off the ceiling. Both of these can use miniature incandescent bulbs or standard length fluorescent tubes, which not only comply with tight energy restrictions, but also provide comfortable, low maintenance light for the entire room.

Lighting Designer
Kenton Knapp and Robert Truax

Interior Designer
Charles Falls

Photographer
Mary Nichols

A series of recessed adjustable fixtures animate this luxurious master bathroom.

Lighting Designer
Ruth Soforenko

Interior Designer
Ruth Soforenko

Photographer
Ron Starr

The Egyptian-inspired wall sconces add a whimsical touch to this well-designed bathroom.

Lighting Designer
Jan Moyer

Photographer
Douglas Salin

Custom fluorescent fixtures create a greenhouse-like feeling for this bright master bathroom.

Lighting Designer
Tom Skradski

Interior Designer
Jane Starr

Photographer
Muffy Kibbey

Recessed adjustable fixtures bring the room's features into prominence while the chandelier takes all the credit.

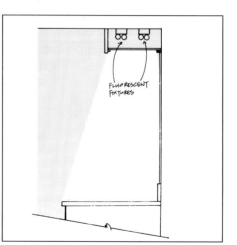

FLUORESCENT
FIXTURES

Lighting Designer
Linda Ferry

Interior Designer
John Schneider

Photographer
Gil Edelstein

Recessed adjustable fixtures add a dramatic flare to this impressive granite bath.

Lighting Designer
Kenton Knapp

Interior Designer
Charles Falls and
Kenton Knapp

Photographer
Eric Zepeda

This sumptuous master bathroom is a sparkly blend of task lighting and ambient illumination. Compact wall bracket fixtures provide the room's fill light, which reduces shadowing on people's faces. The makeup lights surround the mirror to create an even illumination. Recessed lights accent the palm, giving it the appearance of reaching for the skylight above.

Lighting Designer
Catherine Ng and
Randall Whitehead

Interior Designer
Vicky Doubleday and
Peter Gutkin

Photographer
Alan Weintraub

A pendant-hung fixture uses a powerful halogen source suspended below a frosted glass disc to provide the room's fill light. Vertically placed vanity strip fixtures cast a shadowless light for tasks at the sink.

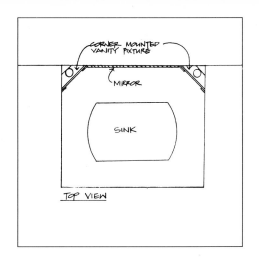

Lighting Designer
Randall Whitehead

Interior Designer
Sarah Lee Roberts

Photographer
Ben Janken

**Incandescent vertically
mounted vanity fixtures
blend beautifully into the
architectural layout of the
bathroom.**

Lighting Designer
Randall Whitehead
and Catherine Ng

Interior Designer
Gary Hutton

Photographer
Ben Janken

**Light fixtures mounted
vertically on either side of
the sink provide the best
illumination for shaving or
applying makeup. Here, the
fixtures are recessed into
the corners so they are
flush with the surface of the
mirrors. These fixtures use
a peach-colored fluorescent
bulb that is very compli-
mentary to skin tones. The
fixtures are dimmable so
the intensity of light can be
changed without greatly
changing the color quality
of the light, as is the case
with incandescent sources.**

Lighting Designer
Randall Whitehead
and Catherine Ng

Interior Designer
Linda Bradshaw-Allen

Photographer
Ben Janken

**The wall sconce mounted
on the mirror makes this
modest bathroom seem
much larger.**

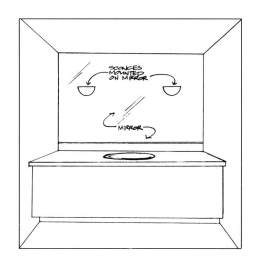

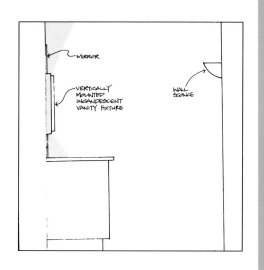

MIRROR

VERTICALLY
MOUNTED
INCANDESCENT
VANITY FIXTURE

WALL
SCONCE

Lighting Designer
Randall Whitehead
and Catherine Ng

Interior Designer
Christian Wright and
Gerald Simpkins

Photographer
Ben Janken

Bathrooms are very task-
oriented so it is important
to have good cross-illumination at the mirror. Wall
sconces (not seen from this
angle) generate the overall
fill light while a torchiere in
the adjoining bedroom
throws a pleasant glow of
illumination into the space.

Lighting Designer
Kenton Knapp

Interior Designer
Charles Falls and Kenton Knapp

Photographer
Patrick Barta

Individual recessed adjustable fixtures bring these American Indian figures dramatic significance.

Lighting Designer
Sherry Scott

Interior Designer
Sherry Scott

Photographer
Michael L. Krasnobrod

This bathroom has space for three people to use the counters simultaneously. The vertical vanity fixtures provide shadowless task light on people's faces for shaving and applying makeup.

Lighting Designer
Sherry Scott

Interior Designer
Sherry Scott

Photographer
Michael L. Krasnobrod

Soft ambient light comes from wall sconces reflecting light off the ceiling in this small but well-designed bathroom.

Answers to Often-Asked Lighting Questions

In my work as a lighting consultant, I often see formal living rooms that look abandoned. "No one ever sits in there," the homeowner tells me. Yet, after we change the lighting, this unused room suddenly becomes the hub of the home. Family and friends gravitate to what is now a warm and inviting place.

Most homeowners are not aware that they can control light and that light affects the mood and function of every room. Lighting can create an ambiance, enhance a work area, and give the illusion of greater depth or scale. The same "psychology" of light used to sell products can be used to show off possessions, highlight art and architecture, or simply make a home brighter and more appealing.

But where do you start? The lighting industry is changing rapidly and more and more new products are appearing. The consumer can get confused. To keep up with the latest advances in design and products, many homeowners — as well as architects, interior designers, and landscapers — are turning to lighting specialists for advice on attractive, energy-efficient, low-maintenance lighting systems. The more you know about lighting, the better you can guide your consultant in creating a lighting design that is right for your home. Here are answers to the most common questions homeowners ask when choosing a lighting system.

Should I install track lighting or recessed lighting?

When track lighting was first introduced, it was considered the answer to all lighting problems. People loved the flexibility and the high-tech look. Only after the novelty wore off did those who had installed track systems begin to notice the drawbacks.

Track is best when it is used for accent lighting to highlight paintings or art objects on walls and tables. It cannot provide adequate fill light (also called ambient light), which is the light that softens and warms a room. When light from a track system falls directly on seating areas, it casts hard shadows on those below. Track lighting is also a poor choice for task lighting for the same reason — you end up working in your own shadow.

Track can work very well as accent lighting especially when there is not enough ceiling depth for recessed lighting or in rental units where cost and portability are important.

Over the past eight years, recessed lighting has greatly improved. Most manufacturers now offer recessed adjustable fixtures that use low-voltage lamps (lamp is the lighting industry's term for a light bulb) and integral transformers (see next section). These fixtures combine the flexibility of track with the clean look of a recessed system. They usually have a 358-degree radius and a 30-degree to 45-degree aiming angle, depending on the manufacturer. A wide variety of beam spreads can be produced simply by changing the lamp. Many of these fixtures are made specifically for remodeling which makes installation into existing ceilings clean and easy.

What is low voltage?

Low voltage, according to electrical code, is anything under 50 volts (normal house current operates at 110-120 volts, also known as line voltage). The most commonly used low-voltage systems are 12 volt and 6 volt. A transformer lowers line voltage to low voltage. It can be located inside the fixture (integral) or somewhere near the fixture (remote).

Low voltage can produce more light per watt than line voltage — often as much as a three-to-one ratio. Although low-voltage systems have a higher initial cost, the advantages in energy efficiency and low maintenance are considerable.

Low-voltage lamps also come in a variety of wattages and beam spreads. You can pinpoint a bowl of flowers or light a 6-foot painting. The most popular of the low-voltage lamps right now is the MR16 (multi-mirror reflector). It is the same type of lamp used in slide projectors. The small size (approximately 2 inches by 2 inches) allows manufacturers to create smaller track fixtures and recessed fixtures with tiny apertures.

How can I get both the color-quality of incandescent light and the energy-efficiency of fluorescent?

For years, the only choice in fluorescent lamps was warm-white or cool-white. The cool-white, as we all probably remember, produced a blue-green light that made people look ghoulish. The warm-white tried to copy

the color of incandescent and got as close as a pinky-orange. Today, there are over 200 colors available in fluorescent. In addition, the technology of fluorescent components has now improved to include a non-humming, full-range dimming ballast line of fixtures.

Are skylights a good idea?

Often skylights are installed to supplement or replace electric lighting during the daytime hours. Clear glass or Plexiglass skylights project a hard beam of light, shaped like the skylight opening, onto the floor. Bronze-colored skylights cast a dimmer version of the same shape. But a white opal acrylic skylight diffuses and softens the natural light producing a more gentle light that fills the space more completely. Existing clear or bronze skylights can be fitted with a white acrylic panel at or above the ceiling line to soften the light they cast.

All skylights should have ultraviolet filters to prevent the sun from rotting or bleaching natural materials. If UV filters are not available from the skylight manufacturer, they often can be found among the stock of companies that

manufacture fluorescent outdoor signs. The original fabricator of these filtering sheets of plastic is Rohm and Haas of Philadelphia. The product is called a UF3 ultraviolet filtering acrylic sheet.

If the light well is deep enough, fluorescent strip lights can be mounted between the acrylic panel and the skylight. These inexpensive strip lights can be used at night to keep the skylight from appearing as a black hole in the ceiling.

How can one avoid glare on shiny dark countertops and backsplashes from under-cabinet fixtures?

This is a common problem and one that is the toughest to solve. Mirror-like finishes reflect everything. One solution is to install a bottom facia piece that shields the fixture from the countertop. The light reflects off the backsplash onto the work surface. The drawback is that much of the light is caught behind the trim piece and never reaches the work surface. A second solution is to install miniature recessed, adjustable low-voltage fixtures in the cabinet. Each fixture would take up the space

about equal to that of a coffee can. These fixtures should be aimed at 45 degree angles to the work surface and louvered to avoid glare.

What is the purpose of recessed incandescent downlighting and when should it not be used?

Recessed fixtures do not provide the best type of general or ambient illumination. Since no light reaches the ceiling, the upper quadrants of the room fall into darkness. This makes the room seem smaller and

creates hard shadows on faces. In California, as stated previously, all general illumination in new kitchens and baths must be fluorescent.

Where should under-cabinet fixtures be placed?

Place task lights at a level between a person's head and the work surface, mounted tight to the face of the cabinet. Have the light reflect off the backsplash and onto the countertop. Shielding should extend 1 inch deeper than the fixture itself. This produces good, shadowless task light.

least energy-efficient. Quartz supplies approximately twice the amount of light provided by household bulbs of the same wattage. Fluorescents give three to five times the amount of incandescent household bulbs of the same wattage.

What are some of the more exciting developments in lighting that can be incorporated into the design?

Neon is fine in situations where there is a good amount of ambient noise, but in quiet areas the inherent hum can be disturbing. The transformer can be remoted to reduce the noise level. Also, be careful with color selection. Intense neon colors can shift the room's color scheme. Local electrical codes should be checked before using neon. In some jurisdictions, they don't permit neon in residential spaces.

Fiber optics provide a subtle glow of light for edge details. The illumination from a fiber optics fixture is even as long as the fiber optic is looped back into the light source or illuminated from both ends. Otherwise, the lighting will be more intense at one end. This is not a

bright source of light. It should serve as a decorative source only. **Backlighting** glass block creates a delightful effect. Remember, you can't light glass block directly as the light simply travels through it and your light source will be visible. You must light whatever wall or surface is behind the glass block to make the block appear illuminated.

Summary

While the new lighting components can achieve spectacular effects, more attention must be paid to lighting design in new construction or remodelling projects.

Choosing the proper fixtures and switching systems is now essential to a cohesive interior environment. If bad decisions are made early in the process, the result can be a chaotic disaster in the look of a room or space (as well as costlier replacements). Conversely, creative decisions timely made will enhance the look of the interior design and architecture in ways that people would never even dream of. Lighting is a powerful tool if people know how to use it.

Where should fixtures above cabinets be placed to achieve good indirect lighting?

Mount fixtures flush with the front of the cabinets, to prevent bright spots and to be sure objects don't block the light. Add a wood block to lift the display items to the facia level so that they are not visually cut off at the bottom.

Where can fixtures be placed to light the interior of a glass door cabinet?

Fixtures can be recessed

above glass shelves. If they are wooden shelves, fixtures can be mounted horizontally on each shelf; or, if the shelves can be set back slightly, the fixtures can be run vertically on the inside edges of the doors.

In high-end, high-budget jobs, do energy considerations still apply?

Whether it's a high-end or an economy project, energy costs should be carefully considered. No one wants to spend more money on energy than is necessary. Incandescent household bulbs are the

Glossary

Absorption

Refers to a measure of the amount of light absorbed by an object instead of being reflected. Dark-colored and matte surfaces are least likely to reflect light.

Accent Lighting

Lighting directed at a particular object in order to focus attention upon it.

Ambient Lighting

The soft indirect light that fills the volume of a room with illumination. It softens shadows on people's faces and creates an inviting glow in the room.

Ballast

Device that converts electrical energy used by fluorescent, mercury vapor, high pressure sodium, or metal halide lamps so the proper amount of power is provided to the lamp.

Beam Spread

The diameter of the circle of light produced by a lamp or lamp and fixture together.

Color Rendering Index

A scale used to measure how well a lamp illuminates an object's color tones as compared with the color of daylight.

Dimming Ballast

Device used for fluorescent lamps to control the light level.

Fluorescent Lamp

A very energy-efficient type of lamp that produces light through the activation of the phosphor coating on the inside surface of a glass envelope. These lamps come in many shapes, wattages, and colors.

Footcandle

A term used to measure the amount of light hitting a surface.

Glare

A source so uncomfortably bright that it becomes the focus of attention rather than what it was meant to illuminate.

High-Intensity Discharge (H.I.D.) Lamp

A category of lamp that emits light through electricity activating pressurized gas in a bulb. Mercury vapor, metal halide, and high-pressure sodium lamps are all H.I.D. lamps. It is a bright and energy-efficient light source used mainly in exterior environments.

High Pressure Sodium

H.I.D. lamp that uses sodium vapor as the light-producing element. It provides a yellow-orange light.

Incandescent Lamp

The traditional type of light bulb that produces light through electricity causing a filament to glow.

Lamp

What the lighting industry technically calls a light bulb. A glass envelope with a gas coating or filament that glows when electricity is applied.

Low-voltage Lighting

System that uses a less than 50-volt current (commonly 12-volt) instead of 120-volt, the standard household current. A transformer is used to convert the electrical power to the appropriate voltage.

Line Voltage

The 120-volt household current, generally standard in North America

Luminaire

The complete light fixture with all parts and lamps (bulbs) necessary for positioning and obtaining power supply.

Mercury Lamp

H.I.D. lamps where light emission is radiated mainly from mercury. They can be clear, phosphor-coated, or self-ballasted. They produce a bluish light.

Metal Halide Lamp

H.I.D. lamps where light comes from radiation from metal halides. It produces the whitest light of the H.I.D. sources.

Mirror Reflector (MR16, MR11)

Miniature tungsten halogen lamps with a variety of beam spreads and wattages

PAR Lamps

Lamps (bulbs) with parabolic aluminized reflectors that give exacting beam control; there are a number of beam patterns to choose from ranging from wide flood to very narrow spot. PAR lamps can be used outdoors due to their thick glass which holds up in severe weather conditions.

Task Lighting

Illumination designed for a work surface so good shadowless light is present.

Transformer

A device which can raise or lower electrical voltage generally used for low-voltage lights.

Tungsten-Halogen

A tungsten incandescent lamp (bulb) containing gas which burns hotter and brighter than standard incandescent lamps.

Directory of Lighting Designers

James Benya, IALD, P.E.
Benya Lighting Design
3491 Cascade Terrace
West Linn, OR 97068
(503)657-9157

Cynthia Bolton-Karasik
The Lighting Group
200 Pine Street #200
San Francisco, CA 94104
(415)989-3446

Gunnar Burklund
1298 Sacramento Street
San Francisco, CA 94108
(415)931-1088

Marcia S. Cox, ASID
Marcia Cox Interiors
133 Stone Pine Lane
Menlo Park, CA 94025
(415)322-4307

Linda Ferry, IESNA, ASID (affiliate)
Architectural Illumination
P.O. Box 2690
Monterey, CA 93942
(408)649-3711

Charles J. Grebmeier, ASID
Grebmeier & Associates
1298 Sacramento Street
San Francisco, CA 94108
(415)931-1088

Susan Huey
Lighting Intergration Technology, Inc.
1747 Scott Street
St. Helena, CA 94574
(707)963-7813

Kenton Knapp, Allied Member ASID
Kenton Knapp Design
P.O. Box 463
Capitola, CA 95010
(408)476-7547

Claudia Librett
Design Studio Inc.
311 East 72nd Street
Penthouse C
New York, NY 10021
(212)772-0521

Donald L. Maxcy, ASID
Donald Maxcy Design Associates
The Union Icehouse
600 East Franklin Street
Monterey, CA 93940
(408)649-6582

Patricia Borba McDonald
McDonald & Moore Ltd.
20 North Almaden Avenue
San Jose, CA 95110
(408)292-6997

Marcia Moore
McDonald & Moore Ltd.
20 North Almaden Avenue
San Jose, CA 95110
(408)292-6997

Janet Lennox Moyer, IALD, IES, ASID
Jan Moyer Design
6225 Chelton Drive
Oakland, CA 94611
(510)482-9193

Catherine Ng, IES
Vice Principal
Light Source
1210 18th Street
San Francisco, CA 94107
(415)626-1210

Pamela Pennington, ASID, IBD
Pamela Pennington Studios
508 Waverley Street
Palo Alto, CA 94301
(415)328-1767

Sherry Scott, ASID
Design Lab
601 4th Street #125
San Francisco, CA 94107
(415)974-1934

Thomas J. Skradski, ASID, IALD
Lumenworks
1121 Ranleigh Way
Suite 100
Piedmont, CA 94610
(510)835-7600

Ruth Soforenko
Ruth Soforenko Associates
137 Forest Avenue
Palo Alto, CA 94301
(415)326-5448

Michael Souter, ASID, IALD
Past President N. Calif. ASID
Luminae Souter Lighting Design
1740 Army Street, 2nd Floor
San Francisco, CA 94124
(415)285-2622

Robert Truax
Robert Truax Lighting Design and
Consultation
360 Arguello Boulevard
San Francisco, CA 94118
(415)668-0253

Randall Whitehead, IALD
Principal
Light Source
1246 18th Street
San Francisco, CA 94107
(415)626-1210

Directory of Photographers

Russell Abraham Photography
60 Federal Street
San Francisco, CA 94107
(415)896-6400

Patrick Barta Photography
80 South Washington Street
Suite 204
Seattle, WA 98104
(206)343-7644

James Benya, IALD, P.E.
Benya Lighting Design
3491 Cascade Terrace
West Linn, OR 97068
(503)657-9157

Gil Edelstein Photography
4120 Matisse Avenue
Woodland Hills, CA 91364
(818)716-8909

Ben Janken Photography
48 Agnon Avenue
San Francisco, CA 94112
(415)206-1645

Muffy Kibbey
4527 Virginia Avenue
Oakland, CA 94619
(510)436-4488

Michael L. Krasnobrod
Fotek
3499 Sacramento Street
San Francisco, CA 94118

Mary Nichols
750 North Stanley Street
Los Angeles, CA 90046
(213)228-2468

Douglas Salin Photography
647 Joost Avenue
San Francisco, CA 94127
(415)584-3322

Durston Saylor
14 East 4th Street
Suite 1118
New York, NY 10012
(212)228-2468

Ron Starr Photography
4104 24th Street #358
San Francisco, CA 94114
(415)541-7732

Alan Weintraub Photography
1832A Mason Street
San Francisco, CA 94133
(415)553-8191

Eric Zepeda
775 Post Street, #610
San Francisco, CA 94109
(415)775-5957